T0275411

Sylvia Plath

The Colossus & Other Poems

Sylvia Plath was born in 1932 in Massachusetts. She began publishing poems and stories as a teenager and by the time she entered Smith College had won several poetry prizes. She was a Fulbright Scholar in Cambridge, England, and married British poet Ted Hughes in London in 1956. The young couple moved to the States, where Plath became an instructor at Smith College. Later, they moved back to England, where Plath continued writing poetry and wrote her novel, *The Bell Jar*, which was first published under the pseudonym Victoria Lucas in England in 1963. On February 11, 1963, Plath committed suicide. Her *Collected Poems*, published posthumously in 1981, won the Pulitzer Prize.

INTERNATIONAL

The Colossus

& Other Poems

by Sylvia Plath

VINTAGE INTERNATIONAL VINTAGE BOOKS
A DIVISION OF RANDOM HOUSE, INC.   NEW YORK

FIRST VINTAGE INTERNATIONAL EDITION, MAY 1998

ISBN: 0-375-70446-9

Random House Web address: www.randomhouse.com

Printed in the United States of America
30 29 28 27 26 25 24 23 22 21

For Ted

ACKNOWLEDGMENTS

Arts in Society, The Atlantic Monthly, Audience, Chelsea, Critical Quarterly, Encounter, Grecourt Review, Harper's Magazine, The Horn Book, The Hudson Review, The Kenyon Review, London Magazine, Mademoiselle, The Nation, The Observer, The Partisan Review, Poetry, The Sewanee Review, The Spectator, The Texas Literary Quarterly, and *The Times Literary Supplement;* also *The New Yorker,* where the following poems originally appeared: "Hardcastle Crags," "Man in Black," "Mussel Hunter at Rock Harbor," and "Watercolor of Grantchester Meadows." I would also like to thank Elizabeth Ames and the Trustees at Yaddo, where many of the poems were written.

CONTENTS

The Manor Garden   3

Two Views of a Cadaver Room   5

Night Shift   7

Sow   9

The Eye-mote   12

Hardcastle Crags   14

Faun   17

Departure   18

The Colossus   20

Lorelei   22

Point Shirley   24

The Bull of Bendylaw   27

All the Dead Dears   29

Aftermath   31

The Thin People   32

Suicide Off Egg Rock   35

Mushrooms   37

I Want, I Want   39

Watercolor of Grantchester Meadows   40

The Ghost's Leavetaking   42

A Winter Ship   44

Full Fathom Five   46

Blue Moles   49

Strumpet Song   51

Man in Black   52

Snakecharmer   54

The Hermit at Outermost House   56

The Disquieting Muses   58

Medallion   61

The Companionable Ills   63

Moonrise   64

Spinster   66

Frog Autumn   68

Mussel Hunter at Rock Harbor   69

The Beekeeper's Daughter   73

The Times Are Tidy   75

The Burnt-out Spa   76

Sculptor   78

Flute Notes from a Reedy Pond   80

The Stones   82

The Colossus

& Other Poems

The Manor Garden

The fountains are dry and the roses over.
Incense of death. Your day approaches.
The pears fatten like little buddhas.
A blue mist is dragging the lake.

You move through the era of fishes,
The smug centuries of the pig—
Head, toe and finger
Come clear of the shadow. History

Nourishes these broken flutings,
These crowns of acanthus,
And the crow settles her garments.
You inherit white heather, a bee's wing,

Two suicides, the family wolves,
Hours of blankness. Some hard stars
Already yellow the heavens.
The spider on its own string

Crosses the lake. The worms
Quit their usual habitations.
The small birds converge, converge
With their gifts to a difficult borning.

Two Views
of a Cadaver Room

1

The day she visited the dissecting room
They had four men laid out, black as burnt turkey,
Already half unstrung. A vinegary fume
Of the death vats clung to them;
The white-smocked boys started working.
The head of his cadaver had caved in,
And she could scarcely make out anything
In that rubble of skull plates and old leather.
A sallow piece of string held it together.

In their jars the snail-nosed babies moon and glow.
He hands her the cut-out heart like a cracked heir-
        loom.

2

In Brueghel's panorama of smoke and slaughter
Two people only are blind to the carrion army:

He, afloat in the sea of her blue satin
Skirts, sings in the direction
Of her bare shoulder, while she bends,
Fingering a leaflet of music, over him,
Both of them deaf to the fiddle in the hands
Of the death's-head shadowing their song.
These Flemish lovers flourish; not for long.

Yet desolation, stalled in paint, spares the little
                country
Foolish, delicate, in the lower right-hand corner.

Night Shift

It was not a heart, beating,
That muted boom, that clangor
Far off, not blood in the ears
Drumming up any fever

To impose on the evening.
The noise came from the outside:
A metal detonating
Native, evidently, to

These stilled suburbs: nobody
Startled at it, though the sound
Shook the ground with its pounding.
It took root at my coming

Till the thudding source, exposed,
Confounded inept guesswork:
Framed in windows of Main Street's
Silver factory, immense

Hammers hoisted, wheels turning,
Stalled, let fall their vertical
Tonnage of metal and wood;
Stunned the marrow. Men in white

Undershirts circled, tending
Without stop those greased machines,
Tending, without stop, the blunt
Indefatigable fact.

Sow

God knows how our neighbor managed to breed
His great sow:
Whatever his shrewd secret, he kept it hid

In the same way
He kept the sow—impounded from public stare,
Prize ribbon and pig show.

But one dusk our questions commended us to a tour
Through his lantern-lit
Maze of barns to the lintel of the sunk sty door

To gape at it:
This was no rose-and-larkspurred china suckling
With a penny slot

For thrifty children, nor dolt pig ripe for heckling,
About to be
Glorified for prime flesh and golden crackling

In a parsley halo;
Nor even one of the common barnyard sows,
Mire-smirched, blowzy,

Maunching thistle and knotweed on her snout-
        cruise—
Bloat tun of milk
On the move, hedged by a litter of feat-foot ninnies

Shrilling her hulk
To halt for a swig at the pink teats. No. This vast
Brobdingnag bulk

Of a sow lounged belly-bedded on that black com-
        post,
Fat-rutted eyes
Dream-filmed. What a vision of ancient hoghood
        must

Thus wholly engross
The great grandam!—our marvel blazoned a knight,
Helmed, in cuirass,

Unhorsed and shredded in the grove of combat
By a grisly-bristled
Boar, fabulous enough to straddle that sow's heat.

But our farmer whistled,
Then, with a jocular fist thwacked the barrel nape,
And the green-copse-castled

Pig hove, letting legend like dried mud drop,
Slowly, grunt
On grunt, up in the flickering light to shape

A monument
Prodigious in gluttonies as that hog whose want
Made lean Lent

Of kitchen slops and, stomaching no constraint,
Proceeded to swill
The seven troughed seas and every earthquaking con-
        tinent.

The Eye-mote

Blameless as daylight I stood looking
At a field of horses, necks bent, manes blown,
Tails streaming against the green
Backdrop of sycamores. Sun was striking
White chapel pinnacles over the roofs,
Holding the horses, the clouds, the leaves

Steadily rooted though they were all flowing
Away to the left like reeds in a sea
When the splinter flew in and stuck my eye,
Needling it dark. Then I was seeing
A melding of shapes in a hot rain:
Horses warped on the altering green,

Outlandish as double-humped camels or uni-
        corns,
Grazing at the margins of a bad monochrome,
Beasts of oasis, a better time.
Abrading my lid, the small grain burns:

Red cinder around which I myself,
Horses, planets and spires revolve.

Neither tears nor the easing flush
Of eyebaths can unseat the speck:
It sticks, and it has stuck a week.
I wear the present itch for flesh,
Blind to what will be and what was.
I dream that I am Oedipus.

What I want back is what I was
Before the bed, before the knife,
Before the brooch-pin and the salve
Fixed me in this parenthesis;
Horses fluent in the wind,
A place, a time gone out of mind.

Hardcastle Crags

Flintlike, her feet struck
Such a racket of echoes from the steely street,
Tacking in moon-blued crooks from the black
Stone-built town, that she heard the quick air
                ignite
Its tinder and shake

A firework of echoes from wall
To wall of the dark, dwarfed cottages.
But the echoes died at her back as the walls
Gave way to fields and the incessant seethe of
                grasses
Riding in the full

Of the moon, manes to the wind,
Tireless, tied, as a moon-bound sea
Moves on its root. Though a mist-wraith
                wound
Up from the fissured valley and hung
                shoulder-high
Ahead, it fattened

To no family-featured ghost,
Nor did any word body with a name
The blank mood she walked in. Once past
The dream-peopled village, her eyes enter-
             tained no dream,
And the sandman's dust

Lost luster under her footsoles.
The long wind, paring her person down
To a pinch of flame, blew its burdened
             whistle
In the whorl of her ear, and like a scooped-out
             pumpkin crown
Her head cupped the babel.

All the night gave her, in return
For the paltry gift of her bulk and the beat
Of her heart was the humped indifferent iron
Of its hills, and its pastures bordered by black
             stone set
On black stone. Barns

Guarded broods and litters
Behind shut doors; the dairy herds
Knelt in the meadow mute as boulders;
Sheep drowsed stoneward in their tussocks of
             wool, and birds,
Twig-sleeping, wore

Granite ruffs, their shadows
The guise of leaves. The whole landscape
Loomed absolute as the antique world was

Once, in its earliest sway of lymph and sap,
Unaltered by eyes,

Enough to snuff the quick
Of her small heat out, but before the weight
Of stones and hills of stones could break
Her down to mere quartz grit in that stony
        light
She turned back.

Faun

Haunched like a faun, he hooed
From grove of moon-glint and fen-frost
Until all owls in the twigged forest
Flapped black to look and brood
On the call this man made.

No sound but a drunken coot
Lurching home along river bank.
Stars hung water-sunk, so a rank
Of double star-eyes lit
Boughs where those owls sat.

An arena of yellow eyes
Watched the changing shape he cut,
Saw hoof harden from foot, saw sprout
Goat-horns. Marked how god rose
And galloped woodward in that guise.

Departure

The figs on the fig tree in the yard are green;
Green, also, the grapes on the green vine
Shading the brickred porch tiles.
The money's run out.

How nature, sensing this, compounds her bitters.
Ungifted, ungrieved, our leavetaking.
The sun shines on unripe corn.
Cats play in the stalks.

Retrospect shall not soften such penury—
Sun's brass, the moon's steely patinas,
The leaden slag of the world—
But always expose

The scraggy rock spit shielding the town's blue bay
Against which the brunt of outer sea
Beats, is brutal endlessly.
Gull-fouled, a stone hut

Bares its low lintel to corroding weathers:
Across that jut of ochreous rock
Goats shamble, morose, rank-haired,
To lick the sea-salt.

The Colossus

I shall never get you put together entirely,
Pieced, glued, and properly jointed.
Mule-bray, pig-grunt and bawdy cackles
Proceed from your great lips.
It's worse than a barnyard.

Perhaps you consider yourself an oracle,
Mouthpiece of the dead, or of some god or
                other.
Thirty years now I have labored
To dredge the silt from your throat.
I am none the wiser.

Scaling little ladders with gluepots and pails
                of lysol
I crawl like an ant in mourning
Over the weedy acres of your brow
To mend the immense skull plates and clear
The bald, white tumuli of your eyes.

A blue sky out of the Oresteia
Arches above us. O father, all by yourself
You are pithy and historical as the Roman
            Forum.
I open my lunch on a hill of black cypress.
Your fluted bones and acanthine hair are
            littered

In their old anarchy to the horizon-line.
It would take more than a lightning-stroke
To create such a ruin.
Nights, I squat in the cornucopia
Of your left ear, out of the wind,

Counting the red stars and those of plum-
            color.
The sun rises under the pillar of your tongue.
My hours are married to shadow.
No longer do I listen for the scrape of a keel
On the blank stones of the landing.

Lorelei

It is no night to drown in:
A full moon, river lapsing
Black beneath bland mirror-sheen,

The blue water-mists dropping
Scrim after scrim like fishnets
Though fishermen are sleeping,

The massive castle turrets
Doubling themselves in a glass
All stillness. Yet these shapes float

Up toward me, troubling the face
Of quiet. From the nadir
They rise, their limbs ponderous

With richness, hair heavier
Than sculpted marble. They sing
Of a world more full and clear

Than can be. Sisters, your song
Bears a burden too weighty
For the whorled ear's listening

Here, in a well-steered country,
Under a balanced ruler.
Deranging by harmony

Beyond the mundane order,
Your voices lay siege. You lodge
On the pitched reefs of nightmare,

Promising sure harborage;
By day, descant from borders
Of hebetude, from the ledge

Also of high windows. Worse
Even than your maddening
Song, your silence. At the source

Of your ice-hearted calling—
Drunkenness of the great depths.
O river, I see drifting

Deep in your flux of silver
Those great goddesses of peace.
Stone, stone, ferry me down there.

Point Shirley

From Water-Tower Hill to the brick prison
The shingle booms, bickering under
The sea's collapse.
Snowcakes break and welter. This year
The gritted wave leaps
The seawall and drops onto a bier
Of quahog chips,
Leaving a salty mash of ice to whiten

In my grandmother's sand yard. She is dead,
Whose laundry snapped and froze here, who
Kept house against
What the sluttish, rutted sea could do.
Squall waves once danced
Ship timbers in through the cellar window;
A thresh-tailed, lanced
Shark littered in the geranium bed—

Such collusion of mulish elements
She wore her broom straws to the nub.

Twenty years out
Of her hand, the house still hugs in each
                drab
Stucco socket
The purple egg-stones: from Great Head's
                knob
To the filled-in Gut
The sea in its cold gizzard ground those
                rounds.

Nobody wintering now behind
The planked-up windows where she set
Her wheat loaves
And apple cakes to cool. What is it
Survives, grieves
So, over this battered, obstinate spit
Of gravel? The waves'
Spewed relics clicker masses in the wind,

Grey waves the stub-necked eiders ride.
A labor of love, and that labor lost.
Steadily the sea
Eats at Point Shirley. She died blessed,
And I come by
Bones, bones only, pawed and tossed,
A dog-faced sea.
The sun sinks under Boston, bloody red.

I would get from these dry-papped stones
The milk your love instilled in them.
The black ducks dive.
And though your graciousness might stream,

And I contrive,
Grandmother, stones are nothing of home
To that spumiest dove.
Against both bar and tower the black sea
runs.

The Bull of Bendylaw

The black bull bellowed before the sea.
The sea, till that day orderly,
Hove up against Bendylaw.

The queen in the mulberry arbor stared
Stiff as a queen on a playing card.
The king fingered his beard.

A blue sea, four horny bull-feet,
A bull-snouted sea that wouldn't stay put,
Bucked at the garden gate.

Along box-lined walks in the florid sun
Toward the rowdy bellow and back again
The lords and ladies ran.

The great bronze gate began to crack,
The sea broke in at every crack,
Pellmell, blueblack.

The bull surged up, the bull surged down,
Not to be stayed by a daisy chain
Nor by any learned man.

O the king's tidy acre is under the sea,
And the royal rose in the bull's belly,
And the bull on the king's highway.

All the Dead Dears

In the Archæological Museum in Cambridge is a stone coffin of the fourth century A.D. containing the skeletons of a woman, a mouse and a shrew. The ankle-bone of the woman has been slightly gnawn.

Rigged poker-stiff on her back
With a granite grin
This antique museum-cased lady
Lies, companioned by the gimcrack
Relics of a mouse and a shrew
That battened for a day on her ankle-bone.

These three, unmasked now, bear
Dry witness
To the gross eating game
We'd wink at if we didn't hear
Stars grinding, crumb by crumb,
Our own grist down to its bony face.

How they grip us through thin and thick,
These barnacle dead!

This lady here's no kin
Of mine, yet kin she is: she'll suck
Blood and whistle my marrow clean
To prove it. As I think now of her head,

From the mercury-backed glass
Mother, grandmother, greatgrandmother
Reach hag hands to haul me in,
And an image looms under the fishpond
        surface
Where the daft father went down
With orange duck-feet winnowing his
        hair—

All the long gone darlings: they
Get back, though, soon,
Soon: be it by wakes, weddings,
Childbirths or a family barbecue:
Any touch, taste, tang's
Fit for those outlaws to ride home on,

And to sanctuary: usurping the armchair
Between tick
And tack of the clock, until we go,
Each skulled-and-crossboned Gulliver
Riddled with ghosts, to lie
Deadlocked with them, taking root as
        cradles rock.

Aftermath

Compelled by calamity's magnet
They loiter and stare as if the house
Burnt-out were theirs, or as if they thought
Some scandal might any minute ooze
From a smoke-choked closet into light;
No deaths, no prodigious injuries
Glut these hunters after an old meat,
Blood-spoor of the austere tragedies.

Mother Medea in a green smock
Moves humbly as any housewife through
Her ruined apartments, taking stock
Of charred shoes, the sodden upholstery:
Cheated of the pyre and the rack,
The crowd sucks her last tear and turns away.

The Thin People

They are always with us, the thin people
Meager of dimension as the grey people

On a movie-screen. They
Are unreal, we say:

It was only in a movie, it was only
In a war making evil headlines when we

Were small that they famished and
Grew so lean and would not round

Out their stalky limbs again though
                peace
Plumped the bellies of the mice

Under the meanest table.
It was during the long hunger-battle

They found their talent to persevere
In thinness, to come, later,

Into our bad dreams, their menace
Not guns, not abuses,

But a thin silence.
Wrapped in flea-ridden donkey skins,

Empty of complaint, forever
Drinking vinegar from tin cups: they
          wore

The insufferable nimbus of the lot-drawn
Scapegoat. But so thin,

So weedy a race could not remain in
          dreams,
Could not remain outlandish victims

In the contracted country of the head
Any more than the old woman in her
          mud hut could

Keep from cutting fat meat
Out of the side of the generous moon
          when it

Set foot nightly in her yard
Until her knife had pared

The moon to a rind of little light.
Now the thin people do not obliterate

Themselves as the dawn
Greyness blues, reddens, and the outline

Of the world comes clear and fills with
        color.
They persist in the sunlit room: the wall-
        paper

Frieze of cabbage-roses and cornflowers
        pales
Under their thin-lipped smiles,

Their withering kingship.
How they prop each other up!

We own no wildernesses rich and deep
        enough
For stronghold against their stiff

Battalions. See, how the tree boles flatten
And lose their good browns

If the thin people simply stand in the
        forest,
Making the world go thin as a wasp's
        nest

And greyer; not even moving their bones.

Suicide Off Egg Rock

Behind him the hotdogs split and drizzled
On the public grills, and the ochreous salt flats,
Gas tanks, factory stacks—that landscape
Of imperfections his bowels were part of—
Rippled and pulsed in the glassy updraft.
Sun struck the water like a damnation.
No pit of shadow to crawl into,
And his blood beating the old tattoo
I am, I am, I am. Children
Were squealing where combers broke and the
         spindrift
Raveled wind-ripped from the crest of the wave.
A mongrel working his legs to a gallop
Hustled a gull flock to flap off the sandspit.

He smoldered, as if stone-deaf, blindfold,
His body beached with the sea's garbage,
A machine to breathe and beat forever.
Flies filing in through a dead skate's eyehole
Buzzed and assailed the vaulted brainchamber.

The words in his book wormed off the pages.
Everything glittered like blank paper.

Everything shrank in the sun's corrosive
Ray but Egg Rock on the blue wastage.
He heard when he walked into the water

The forgetful surf creaming on those ledges.

Mushrooms

Overnight, very
Whitely, discreetly,
Very quietly

Our toes, our noses
Take hold on the loam,
Acquire the air.

Nobody sees us,
Stops us, betrays us;
The small grains make room.

Soft fists insist on
Heaving the needles,
The leafy bedding,

Even the paving.
Our hammers, our rams,
Earless and eyeless,

Perfectly voiceless,
Widen the crannies,
Shoulder through holes. We

Diet on water,
On crumbs of shadow,
Bland-mannered, asking

Little or nothing.
So many of us!
So many of us!

We are shelves, we are
Tables, we are meek,
We are edible,

Nudgers and shovers
In spite of ourselves.
Our kind multiplies:

We shall by morning
Inherit the earth.
Our foot's in the door.

I Want, I Want

Open-mouthed, the baby god
Immense, bald, though baby-headed,
Cried out for the mother's dug.
The dry volcanoes cracked and spit,

Sand abraded the milkless lip.
Cried then for the father's blood
Who set wasp, wolf and shark to work,
Engineered the gannet's beak.

Dry-eyed, the inveterate patriarch
Raised his men of skin and bone,
Barbs on the crown of gilded wire,
Thorns on the bloody rose-stem.

Watercolor of Grantchester Meadows

━━━━━━

There, spring lambs jam the sheepfold. In air
Stilled, silvered as water in a glass
Nothing is big or far.
The small shrew chitters from its wilderness
Of grassheads and is heard.
Each thumb-size bird
Flits nimble-winged in thickets, and of good color.

Cloudrack and owl-hollowed willows slanting over
The bland Granta double their white and green
World under the sheer water
And ride that flux at anchor, upside down.
The punter sinks his pole.
In Byron's pool
Cattails part where the tame cygnets steer.

It is a country on a nursery plate.
Spotted cows revolve their jaws and crop

Red clover or gnaw beetroot
Bellied on a nimbus of sun-glazed buttercup.
Hedging meadows of benign
Arcadian green
The blood-berried hawthorn hides its spines with
          white.

Droll, vegetarian, the water rat
Saws down a reed and swims from his limber grove,
While the students stroll or sit,
Hands laced, in a moony indolence of love—
Black-gowned, but unaware
How in such mild air
The owl shall stoop from his turret, the rat cry out.

The Ghost's Leavetaking

Enter the chilly no-man's land of about
Five o'clock in the morning, the no-color void
Where the waking head rubbishes out the draggled
      lot
Of sulfurous dreamscapes and obscure lunar conun-
      drums
Which seemed, when dreamed, to mean so pro-
      foundly much,

Gets ready to face the ready-made creation
Of chairs and bureaus and sleep-twisted sheets.
This is the kingdom of the fading apparition,
The oracular ghost who dwindles on pin-legs
To a knot of laundry, with a classic bunch of sheets

Upraised, as a hand, emblematic of farewell.
At this joint between two worlds and two entirely
Incompatible modes of time, the raw material
Of our meat-and-potato thoughts assumes the
      nimbus
Of ambrosial revelation. And so departs.

Chair and bureau are the hieroglyphs
Of some godly utterance wakened heads ignore:
So these posed sheets, before they thin to nothing,
Speak in sign language of a lost otherworld,
A world we lose by merely waking up.

Trailing its telltale tatters only at the outermost
Fringe of mundane vision, this ghost goes
Hand aloft, goodbye, goodbye, not down
Into the rocky gizzard of the earth,
But toward a region where our thick atmosphere

Diminishes, and God knows what is there.
A point of exclamation marks that sky
In ringing orange like a stellar carrot.
Its round period, displaced and green,
Suspends beside it the first point, the starting

Point of Eden, next the new moon's curve.
Go, ghost of our mother and father, ghost of us,
And ghost of our dreams' children, in those sheets
Which signify our origin and end,
To the cloud-cuckoo land of color wheels

And pristine alphabets and cows that moo
And moo as they jump over moons as new
As that crisp cusp toward which you voyage now.
Hail and farewell. Hello, goodbye. O keeper
Of the profane grail, the dreaming skull.

A Winter Ship

━━━━━━━

At this wharf there are no grand landings to
        speak of.
Red and orange barges list and blister
Shackled to the dock, outmoded, gaudy,
And apparently indestructible.
The sea pulses under a skin of oil.

A gull holds his pose on a shanty ridgepole,
Riding the tide of the wind, steady
As wood and formal, in a jacket of ashes,
The whole flat harbor anchored in
The round of his yellow eye-button.

A blimp swims up like a day-moon or tin
Cigar over his rink of fishes.
The prospect is dull as an old etching.
They are unloading three barrels of little crabs.
The pier pilings seem about to collapse

And with them that rickety edifice
Of warehouses, derricks, smokestacks and bridges

In the distance. All around us the water slips
And gossips in its loose vernacular,
Ferrying the smells of dead cod and tar.

Farther out, the waves will be mouthing icecakes—
A poor month for park-sleepers and lovers.
Even our shadows are blue with cold.
We wanted to see the sun come up
And are met, instead, by this iceribbed ship,

Bearded and blown, an albatross of frost,
Relic of tough weather, every winch and stay
Encased in a glassy pellicle.
The sun will diminish it soon enough:
Each wave-tip glitters like a knife.

Full Fathom Five

Old man, you surface seldom.
Then you come in with the tide's
        coming
When seas wash cold, foam-

Capped: white hair, white beard,
        far-flung,
A dragnet, rising, falling, as waves
Crest and trough. Miles long

Extend the radial sheaves
Of your spread hair, in which wrin-
        kling skeins
Knotted, caught, survives

The old myth of origins
Unimaginable. You float near
As keeled ice-mountains

Of the north, to be steered clear
Of, not fathomed. All obscurity
Starts with a danger:

Your dangers are many. I
Cannot look much but your form
           suffers
Some strange injury

And seems to die: so vapors
Ravel to clearness on the dawn sea.
The muddy rumors

Of your burial move me
To half-believe: your reappearance
Proves rumors shallow,

For the archaic trenched lines
Of your grained face shed time in
           runnels:
Ages beat like rains

On the unbeaten channels
Of the ocean. Such sage humor
           and
Durance are whirlpools

To make away with the ground-
Work of the earth and the sky's
           ridgepole.
Waist down, you may wind

One labyrinthine tangle
To root deep among knuckles, shin-
            bones,
Skulls. Inscrutable,

Below shoulders not once
Seen by any man who kept his head,
You defy questions;

You defy other godhood.
I walk dry on your kingdom's border
Exiled to no good.

Your shelled bed I remember.
Father, this thick air is murderous.
I would breathe water.

Blue Moles

1

They're out of the dark's ragbag, these two
Moles dead in the pebbled rut,
Shapeless as flung gloves, a few feet apart—
Blue suede a dog or fox has chewed.
One, by himself, seemed pitiable enough,
Little victim unearthed by some large crea-
          ture
From his orbit under the elm root.
The second carcass makes a duel of the
          affair:
Blind twins bitten by bad nature.

The sky's far dome is sane and clear.
Leaves, undoing their yellow caves
Between the road and the lake water,
Bare no sinister spaces. Already
The moles look neutral as the stones.
Their corkscrew noses, their white hands
Uplifted, stiffen in a family pose.

49

Difficult to imagine how fury struck—
Dissolved now, smoke of an old war.

2

Nightly the battle-shouts start up
In the ear of the veteran, and again
I enter the soft pelt of the mole.
Light's death to them: they shrivel in it.
They move through their mute rooms while
          I sleep,
Palming the earth aside, grubbers
After the fat children of root and rock.
By day, only the topsoil heaves.
Down there one is alone.

Outsize hands prepare a path,
They go before: opening the veins,
Delving for the appendages
Of beetles, sweetbreads, shards—to be
          eaten
Over and over. And still the heaven
Of final surfeit is just as far
From the door as ever. What happens be-
          tween us
Happens in darkness, vanishes
Easy and often as each breath.

Strumpet Song

With white frost gone
And all green dreams not worth much,
After a lean day's work
Time comes round for that foul slut:
Mere bruit of her takes our street
Until every man,
Red, pale or dark,
Veers to her slouch.

Mark, I cry, that mouth
Made to do violence on,
That seamed face
Askew with blotch, dint, scar
Struck by each dour year.
Walks there not some such one man
As can spare breath
To patch with brand of love this rank grimace
Which out from black tarn, ditch and cup
Into my most chaste own eyes
Looks up.

Man in Black

Where the three magenta
Breakwaters take the shove
And suck of the grey sea

To the left, and the wave
Unfists against the dun
Barb-wired headland of

The Deer Island prison
With its trim piggeries,
Hen huts and cattle green

To the right, and March ice
Glazes the rock pools yet,
Snuff-colored sand cliffs rise

Over a great stone spit
Bared by each falling tide,
And you, across those white

Stones, strode out in your dead
Black coat, black shoes, and your
Black hair till there you stood,

Fixed vortex on the far
Tip, riveting stones, air,
All of it, together.

Snakecharmer

As the gods began one world, and man another,
So the snakecharmer begins a snaky sphere
With moon-eye, mouth-pipe. He pipes. Pipes green.
      Pipes water.

Pipes water green until green waters waver
With reedy lengths and necks and undulatings.
And as his notes twine green, the green river

Shapes its images around his songs.
He pipes a place to stand on, but no rocks,
No floor: a wave of flickering grass tongues

Supports his foot. He pipes a world of snakes,
Of sways and coilings, from the snake-rooted bottom
Of his mind. And now nothing but snakes

Is visible. The snake-scales have become
Leaf, become eyelid; snake-bodies, bough, breast
Of tree and human. And he within this snakedom

Rules the writhings which make manifest
His snakehood and his might with pliant tunes
From his thin pipe. Out of this green nest

As out of Eden's navel twist the lines
Of snaky generations: let there be snakes!
And snakes there were, are, will be—till yawns

Consume this piper and he tires of music
And pipes the world back to the simple fabric
Of snake-warp, snake-weft. Pipes the cloth of snakes

To a melting of green waters, till no snake
Shows its head, and those green waters back to
Water, to green, to nothing like a snake.
Puts up his pipe, and lids his moony eye.

The Hermit
at Outermost House

Sky and sea, horizon-hinged
Tablets of blank blue, couldn't,
Clapped shut, flatten this man out.

The great gods, Stone-Head, Claw-
        Foot,
Winded by much rock-bumping
And claw-threat, realized that.

For what, then, had they endured
Dourly the long hots and colds,
Those old despots, if he sat

Laugh-shaken on his doorsill,
Backbone unbendable as
Timbers of his upright hut?

Hard gods were there, nothing else.
Still he thumbed out something else.
Thumbed no stony, horny pot,

But a certain meaning green.
He withstood them, that hermit.
Rock-face, crab-claw verged on
            green.

Gulls mulled in the greenest light.

The Disquieting Muses

Mother, mother, what illbred aunt
Or what disfigured and unsightly
Cousin did you so unwisely keep
Unasked to my christening, that she
Sent these ladies in her stead
With heads like darning-eggs to nod
And nod and nod at foot and head
And at the left side of my crib?

Mother, who made to order stories
Of Mixie Blackshort the heroic bear,
Mother, whose witches always, always
Got baked into gingerbread, I wonder
Whether you saw them, whether you said
Words to rid me of those three ladies
Nodding by night around my bed,
Mouthless, eyeless, with stitched bald
        head.

In the hurricane, when father's twelve
Study windows bellied in

Like bubbles about to break, you fed
My brother and me cookies and Ovaltine
And helped the two of us to choir:
"Thor is angry: boom boom boom!
Thor is angry: we don't care!"
But those ladies broke the panes.

When on tiptoe the schoolgirls danced,
Blinking flashlights like fireflies
And singing the glowworm song, I could
Not lift a foot in the twinkle-dress
But, heavy-footed, stood aside
In the shadow cast by my dismal-headed
Godmothers, and you cried and cried:
And the shadow stretched, the lights
                    went out.

Mother, you sent me to piano lessons
And praised my arabesques and trills
Although each teacher found my touch
Oddly wooden in spite of scales
And the hours of practicing, my ear
Tone-deaf and yes, unteachable.
I learned, I learned, I learned elsewhere,
From muses unhired by you, dear
                    mother,

I woke one day to see you, mother,
Floating above me in bluest air
On a green balloon bright with a million
Flowers and bluebirds that never were
Never, never, found anywhere.

But the little planet bobbed away
Like a soap-bubble as you called: Come
        here!
And I faced my traveling companions.

Day now, night now, at head, side, feet,
They stand their vigil in gowns of stone,
Faces blank as the day I was born,
Their shadows long in the setting sun
That never brightens or goes down.
And this is the kingdom you bore me to,
Mother, mother. But no frown of mine
Will betray the company I keep.

Medallion

By the gate with star and moon
Worked into the peeled orange
                wood
The bronze snake lay in the sun

Inert as a shoelace; dead
But pliable still, his jaw
Unhinged and his grin crooked,

Tongue a rose-colored arrow.
Over my hand I hung him.
His little vermilion eye

Ignited with a glassed flame
As I turned him in the light;
When I split a rock one time

The garnet bits burned like
                that.
Dust dulled his back to ocher
The way sun ruins a trout.

Yet his belly kept its fire
Going under the chainmail,
The old jewels smoldering there

In each opaque belly-scale:
Sunset looked at through milk
                glass.
And I saw white maggots coil

Thin as pins in the dark bruise
Where his innards bulged as if
He were digesting a mouse.

Knifelike, he was chaste enough,
Pure death's-metal. The yard-
                man's
Flung brick perfected his laugh.

The Companionable Ills

The nose-end that twitches, the
            old imperfections—
Tolerable now as moles on the
            face
Put up with until chagrin gives
            place
To a wry complaisance—

Dug in first as God's spurs
To start the spirit out of the
            mud
It stabled in; long-used, became
            well-loved
Bedfellows of the spirit's de-
            bauch, fond masters.

Moonrise

Grub-white mulberries redden among leaves.
I'll go out and sit in white like they do,
Doing nothing. July's juice rounds their nubs.

This park is fleshed with idiot petals.
White catalpa flowers tower, topple,
Cast a round white shadow in their dying.

A pigeon rudders down. Its fantail's white.
Vocation enough: opening, shutting
White petals, white fantails, ten white fingers.

Enough for fingernails to make half-moons
Redden in white palms no labor reddens.
White bruises toward color, else collapses.

Berries redden. A body of whiteness
Rots, and smells of rot under its headstone
Though the body walk out in clean linen.

I smell that whiteness here, beneath the
        stones
Where small ants roll their eggs, where grubs
        fatten.
Death may whiten in sun or out of it.

Death whitens in the egg and out of it.
I can see no color for this whiteness.
White: it is a complexion of the mind.

I tire, imagining white Niagaras
Build up from a rock root, as fountains build
Against the weighty image of their fall.

Lucina, bony mother, laboring
Among the socketed white stars, your face
Of candor pares white flesh to the white
        bone,

Who drag our ancient father at the heel,
White-bearded, weary. The berries purple
And bleed. The white stomach may ripen yet.

Spinster

Now this particular girl
During a ceremonious April walk
With her latest suitor
Found herself, of a sudden, intolerably struck
By the birds' irregular babel
And the leaves' litter.

By this tumult afflicted, she
Observed her lover's gestures unbalance the air,
His gait stray uneven
Through a rank wilderness of fern and flower.
She judged petals in disarray,
The whole season, sloven.

How she longed for winter then!—
Scrupulously austere in its order
Of white and black
Ice and rock, each sentiment within border,
And heart's frosty discipline
Exact as a snowflake.

But here—a burgeoning
Unruly enough to pitch her five queenly wits
Into vulgar motley—
A treason not to be borne. Let idiots
Reel giddy in bedlam spring:
She withdrew neatly.

And round her house she set
Such a barricade of barb and check
Against mutinous weather
As no mere insurgent man could hope to break
With curse, fist, threat
Or love, either.

Frog Autumn

Summer grows old, cold-blooded mother.
The insects are scant, skinny.
In these palustral homes we only
Croak and wither.

Mornings dissipate in somnolence.
The sun brightens tardily
Among the pithless reeds. Flies fail us.
The fen sickens.

Frost drops even the spider. Clearly
The genius of plenitude
Houses himself elsewhere. Our folk thin
Lamentably.

Mussel Hunter
at Rock Harbor

I came before the water-
Colorists came to get the
Good of the Cape light that scours
Sand grit to sided crystal
And buffs and sleeks the blunt hulls
Of the three fishing smacks beached
On the bank of the river's

Backtracking tail. I'd come for
Free fish-bait: the blue mussels
Clumped like bulbs at the grass-
        root
Margin of the tidal pools.
Dawn tide stood dead low. I smelt
Mud stench, shell guts, gulls'
        leavings;
Heard a queer crusty scrabble

Cease, and I neared the silenced
Edge of a cratered pool-bed.
The mussels hung dull blue and
Conspicuous, yet it seemed
A sly world's hinges had swung
Shut against me. All held still.
Though I counted scant seconds,

Enough ages lapsed to win
Confidence of safe-conduct
In the wary otherworld
Eyeing me. Grass put forth claws;
Small mud knobs, nudged from
                    under,
Displaced their domes as tiny
Knights might doff their casques.
                    The crabs

Inched from their pygmy burrows
And from the trench-dug mud, all
Camouflaged in mottled mail
Of browns and greens. Each wore
                    one
Claw swollen to a shield large
As itself—no fiddler's arm
Grown Gargantuan by trade,

But grown grimly, and grimly
Borne, for a use beyond my
Guessing of it. Sibilant
Mass-motived hordes, they sidled
Out in a converging stream

Toward the pool-mouth, perhaps to
Meet the thin and sluggish thread

Of sea retracing its tide-
Way up the river-basin.
Or to avoid me. They moved
Obliquely with a dry-wet
Sound, with a glittery wisp
And trickle. Could they feel mud
Pleasurable under claws

As I could between bare toes?
That question ended it—I
Stood shut out, for once, for all,
Puzzling the passage of their
Absolutely alien
Order as I might puzzle
At the clear tail of Halley's

Comet coolly giving my
Orbit the go-by, made known
By a family name it
Knew nothing of. So the crabs
Went about their business, which
Wasn't fiddling, and I filled
A big handkerchief with blue

Mussels. From what the crabs saw,
If they could see, I was one
Two-legged mussel-picker.
High on the airy thatching
Of the dense grasses I found

The husk of a fiddler-crab,
Intact, strangely strayed above

His world of mud—green color
And innards bleached and blown off
Somewhere by much sun and wind;
There was no telling if he'd
Died recluse or suicide
Or headstrong Columbus crab.
The crab-face, etched and set there,

Grimaced as skulls grimace: it
Had an Oriental look,
A samurai death mask done
On a tiger tooth, less for
Art's sake than God's. Far from
        sea—
Where red-freckled crab-backs, claws
And whole crabs, dead, their soggy

Bellies pallid and upturned,
Perform their shambling waltzes
On the waves' dissolving turn
And return, losing themselves
Bit by bit to their friendly
Element—this relic saved
Face, to face the bald-faced sun.

The Beekeeper's Daughter

A garden of mouthings. Purple, scarlet-speckled,
       black
The great corollas dilate, peeling back their silks.
Their musk encroaches, circle after circle,
A well of scents almost too dense to breathe in.
Hieratical in your frock coat, maestro of the bees,
You move among the many-breasted hives,

My heart under your foot, sister of a stone.

Trumpet-throats open to the beaks of birds.
The Golden Rain Tree drips its powders down.
In these little boudoirs streaked with orange and red
The anthers nod their heads, potent as kings
To father dynasties. The air is rich.
Here is a queenship no mother can contest—

A fruit that's death to taste: dark flesh, dark parings.

In burrows narrow as a finger, solitary bees
Keep house among the grasses. Kneeling down

I set my eye to a hole-mouth and meet an eye
Round, green, disconsolate as a tear.
Father, bridegroom, in this Easter egg
Under the coronal of sugar roses

The queen bee marries the winter of your year.

The Times Are Tidy

Unlucky the hero born
In this province of the stuck record
Where the most watchful cooks go
        jobless
And the mayor's rôtisserie turns
Round of its own accord.

There's no career in the venture
Of riding against the lizard,
Himself withered these latter-days
To leaf-size from lack of action:
History's beaten the hazard.

The last crone got burnt up
More than eight decades back
With the love-hot herb, the talking cat,
But the children are better for it,
The cow milk's cream an inch thick.

The Burnt-out Spa

An old beast ended in this place:

A monster of wood and rusty teeth.
Fire smelted his eyes to lumps
Of pale blue vitreous stuff, opaque
As resin drops oozed from pine bark.

The rafters and struts of his body wear
Their char of karakul still. I can't tell
How long his carcass has foundered
          under
The rubbish of summers, the black-
          leaved falls.

Now little weeds insinuate
Soft suede tongues between his bones.
His armorplate, his toppled stones
Are an esplanade for crickets.

I pick and pry like a doctor or
Archæologist among
Iron entrails, enamel bowls,
The coils and pipes that made him
          run.

The small dell eats what ate it once.
And yet the ichor of the spring
Proceeds clear as it ever did
From the broken throat, the
          marshy lip.

It flows off below the green and white
Balustrade of a sag-backed bridge.
Leaning over, I encounter one
Blue and improbable person

Framed in a basketwork of cattails.
O she is gracious and austere,
Seated beneath the toneless water!
It is not I, it is not I.

No animal spoils on her green door-
          step.
And we shall never enter there
Where the durable ones keep house.
The stream that hustles us

Neither nourishes nor heals.

Sculptor

FOR LEONARD BASKIN

To his house the bodiless
Come to barter endlessly
Vision, wisdom, for bodies
Palpable as his, and weighty.

Hands moving move priestlier
Than priest's hands, invoke no
                    vain
Images of light and air
But sure stations in bronze,
            wood, stone.

Obdurate, in dense-grained
            wood,
A bald angel blocks and shapes
The flimsy light; arms folded
Watches his cumbrous world
            eclipse

Inane worlds of wind and cloud.
Bronze dead dominate the floor,
Resistive, ruddy-bodied,
Dwarfing us. Our bodies flicker

Toward extinction in those eyes
Which, without him, were beg-
                    gared
Of place, time, and their bodies.
Emulous spirits make discord,

Try entry, enter nightmares
Until his chisel bequeaths
Them life livelier than ours,
A solider repose than death's.

Flute Notes
from a Reedy Pond

Now coldness comes sifting down, layer after layer,
To our bower at the lily root.
Overhead the old umbrellas of summer
Wither like pithless hands. There is little shelter.

Hourly the eye of the sky enlarges its blank
Dominion. The stars are no nearer.
Already frog-mouth and fish-mouth drink
The liquor of indolence, and all things sink

Into a soft caul of forgetfulness.
The fugitive colors die.
Caddis worms drowse in their silk cases,
The lamp-headed nymphs are nodding to sleep like
     statues.

Puppets, loosed from the strings of the puppet-
     master,

Wear masks of horn to bed.
This is not death, it is something safer.
The wingy myths won't tug at us any more:

The molts are tongueless that sang from above the
                        water
Of golgotha at the tip of a reed,
And how a god flimsy as a baby's finger
Shall unhusk himself and steer into the air.

The Stones

This is the city where men are mended.
I lie on a great anvil.
The flat blue sky-circle

Flew off like the hat of a doll
When I fell out of the light. I entered
The stomach of indifference, the wordless cupboard.

The mother of pestles diminished me.
I became a still pebble.
The stones of the belly were peaceable,

The head-stone quiet, jostled by nothing.
Only the mouth-hole piped out,
Importunate cricket

In a quarry of silences.
The people of the city heard it.
They hunted the stones, taciturn and separate,

The mouth-hole crying their locations.
Drunk as a fetus
I suck at the paps of darkness.

The food tubes embrace me. Sponges kiss my lichens
            away.
The jewelmaster drives his chisel to pry
Open one stone eye.

This is the after-hell: I see the light.
A wind unstoppers the chamber
Of the ear, old worrier.

Water mollifies the flint lip,
And daylight lays its sameness on the wall.
The grafters are cheerful,

Heating the pincers, hoisting the delicate hammers.
A current agitates the wires
Volt upon volt. Catgut stitches my fissures.

A workman walks by carrying a pink torso.
The storerooms are full of hearts.
This is the city of spare parts.

My swaddled legs and arms smell sweet as rubber.
Here they can doctor heads, or any limb.
On Fridays the little children come

To trade their hooks for hands.
Dead men leave eyes for others.
Love is the uniform of my bald nurse.

Love is the bone and sinew of my curse.
The vase, reconstructed, houses
The elusive rose.

Ten fingers shape a bowl for shadows.
My mendings itch. There is nothing to do.
I shall be good as new.